GW00865454

Life. Changes. Quick.

Get stupid rich, have a six-pack and fall in love;
all by this time next year.

Johnny F.D.
www.LifeChangesQuick.com

Copyright and Disclaimers

Life. Changes. Quick.
By Johnny F.D.

Copyright 2014
All Rights Reserved

Gratitude:
To my editor Russell Walker for volunteering to fix 12 Weeks in Thailand and then again with Life Changes Quick. We've never met, yet you've helped more people than you know. To my friends and family, even if we may not always see eye to eye, at the end of the day, love trumps it all. To my girlfriend for putting up with me and loving me. To my mentors who have made both this book and this life possible. From the bottom of my heart, thank you.

To the people who say I have inspired them,
you are the ones that have inspired me to write this book.

Table of Contents

Introduction.

I thought I had finally figured it out. I managed to get the courage to quit my job, moved to a tropical island and somehow got paid to drink beers on the beach, go scuba diving and practice Muay Thai all day. It was a dream come true and it all started with a short three week vacation to Thailand in 2008.

I talked about it in my first book, 12 Weeks in Thailand: The Good Life on the Cheap. I went into detail on how I quit my corporate job in California, but just in case you haven't read it yet: I moved to Thailand a few years ago and got by on what little savings I had. I didn't speak the language, know a single person in the country or have any source of income at the time. I just knew that I was stressed out in the U.S., so I decided to risk it all for the ultimate payoff.

Up until that point in life, I had done everything I was supposed to do: I graduated from university with honors, got a good job with a big American corporation and lived in a big house in one of the best cities in the States. I didn't realize until I had moved to Thailand what I was missing and to sum it all up, it was freedom.

It's ironic that I had to leave the United States of America - the country that prides itself on freedom - to really feel it. I realized that freedom wasn't simply being able to vote, drive a big car, or own guns. Freedom to me was being able to do what I loved everyday without having stress, traffic to contend with, responsibilities or bills to pay, and to finally be happy.

Moving to Thailand instantly gave me the freedom to live a good, comfortable life without worry, which was something I didn't even know actually existed, but once I had a taste of it, I couldn't imagine living without it. Then it all hit me. After four years of doing whatever I wanted and living a great life in Thailand, waking up on steps from the beach, after a night of drinking beers on the sand, I suddenly realized that I had been lying to myself and building another prison around my new seemingly carefree life.

It all came to me when my friend mentioned he was moving to Europe for the summer, with no other reason than Europe was nice during the those months.

It was at that instant I realized I was only content in my new life but was trapped living in cheap places and didn't really have as much freedom as I previously thought. I had gained a lot of weight from drinking one too many Pina Coladas, stopped exploring and sightseeing and, even though I had my share of flings with resort guests, I was single and lonelier than ever. I had stopped being happy long ago but had gotten content once again. I used to dream about being content and had finally achieved it, not realizing it was holding me back from happiness.

My life became a lie. I had stopped loving both scuba diving and Muay Thai as I no longer did them out of passion. Don't get me wrong, for the first few months, even years, it was the best experience in the world. I lived on a resort, got paid to teach people what I loved and to share in their joy and frustrations alike; however, at some point, the joy diminished and all I felt was the frustration. I was never that good at Muay Thai and even though I loved it, I knew deep down inside it wasn't a career.

As for diving, I worked as an instructor for years and was pretty damn good at it. But imagine being a car enthusiast and only working with new student drivers day in and day out. That is exactly how I started to feel but there was nothing I could do about it. I had spent thousands of dollars going through the certifications to become a dive instructor and was now stuck with it as my only means of income.

To make things worse I was out of savings, didn't have a plane ticket home or a job to go back to.

My friends and family, who I thought would have been happy for me all of these years for pursuing my passions and going after my dreams, would finally get to say, "I told you so."

I had made the mistake and assumed everyone I knew would want to see how happy I was and support my decision to move. Instead, I noticed that people were secretly hoping that this lifestyle would fail and eventually go back to the real world. I knew I had given it my best shot, enjoyed four years of traveling and seeing the world, I didn't want to just give up and return to the real world.

The thought of moving back home, interviewing for jobs again, even having to move back in with my parents while I got back on my feet, made me desperate to find a solution. Having my back against the wall, I knew I was approaching the end of the line. I asked myself what I had accomplished since then and what would really make the entire journey worth it. I asked myself what the one goal I had never accomplished was.

As it turns out, it was quite simple.

Chapter 1: Going Home With Something To Show

I was running out of money, had no career or backup plan and, as ridiculous as it may sound, the most important thing on my mind wasn't getting a job or even starting a business. It was getting in shape. I figured, even if everything else failed, as long as I went back home in shape, at least I would have something to show for it.

I know it seems vain (and it was) but that initial goal started a snowball of success in all other aspects of my life. It was also the only thing I really had control over at the time. I had no idea how to build a business, or start anything meaningful but I knew that I had the knowledge to get in shape, I just needed to finally put forth the dedication.

Ever since I was a teenager, being a chubby kid with no muscle, I'd wanted to get in shape. I convinced my dad to take me to the local Big 5 Sporting Goods store to buy my first set of dumbbells; they weighed 10 lbs each and were secondhand. I still have them today under my bed at my parents' house and if I knew then what I know now (about diet, health and exercise) those are the only weights I would have ever needed to be in decent shape today.

The goal was simple: I wanted to return home with a Six Pack, something that I've never even been close to accomplishing before.

I told myself that this is it. I'm at a turning point of my life and I'm not getting any younger. At almost 32 years of age I knew that life could all go downhill from here or back up. Little did I know that once you get over the mountain, all of a sudden you see a panorama of opportunities on the other side.

Most people, however, assume once you reach the top - once you get in the best shape of your life and make it to the summit of the mountain - that you simply plant your flag, say you did it and come back down. Those people are wrong. Once you make it, you get accepted to a club with unending benefits and you'll want to stay there. But even without knowing what else reaching the top gives you, I vowed to do it. I was desperate for some form of success in my life. I didn't want to return back to the U.S. four years older, completely broke and with nothing to show for it.

During that time my friends had gotten married, started families and furthered their careers.

I knew that with each year that passed it would become more difficult to get in good physical shape: my body was getting older, less resilient and my natural testosterone production slowed down. I knew that if I went back to the U.S. and got a normal job, I wouldn't have the time or energy to focus on my fitness dreams. They would have remained just that - dreams. This was it and, quite possibly, the last time in my life I'd have the chance to summit my mountain. So I vowed to do it, no matter what.

The photo above is of me actually summiting a mountain. I climbed Mt. Kinabalu, the highest peak in South East Asia at 4,000m during my travels. However, all the running, hiking and cardio I did to prepare for it, the daily training from living at a Muay Thai gym and even the 8,000

calories I burned physically climbing it wasn't enough to get me visible abs.

My goal was to spend an entire year working towards my fitness goals, no matter the cost. I asked myself: if I woke up on my 33rd birthday with no money in the bank, no career, no girlfriend, no social life or other accomplishments would I be happy as long as I was in shape?

The answer was yes, heck yes!

Chapter 2: Drinking The CrossFit Kool-Aid

"The things that get measured are the things that get done." - Michael LeBoeuf

It was during my quest for vanity that I came to meet a guy named Kurt. He was tall, good looking, in great shape and he would take home girls every weeknight back to his rooftop pool. I was envious. He had everything that I thought I wanted.

We met at CrossFit. I had initially heard of the CrossFit cult years ago when I still lived in Los Angeles. The only three things I had ever heard about it were that it worked, its members were obsessive about it and that it was (outrageously) expensive. I even decided to give it a shot once but when I saw the $250 a month membership fee I brushed it off and never thought about it again. Luckily, one of the female fighters at my Muay Thai gym had started going to one in Thailand and this replanted a seed into my mind to give it another try.

At the time I had just completed my sixth professional fight and lost. I've never told this to anyone but the night before the fight my back locked up and I could hardly move. It's happened to me a few times in the past and I got over it by self-medicating with muscle relaxers and pain pills while sleeping on a flat wooden bench.

I woke up the day of the fight a bit woozy but didn't want to pull out. I felt slow, out of shape and was exhausted by the time I stepped into the ring. I tried my best but ultimately lost to points after a grueling five round decision. I went home that night knowing that what little chance I had at being a pro-fighter was over. My heart and mind wasn't in it, and all I had to show for it was a host of injuries.

The good thing that came out of it, though, was I decided that if I were ever to fight again, I would be 30lbs lighter. It was then that I decided to dedicate to CrossFit.

Goal #1 Workout Five Days A Week.

Luckily, most things in Thailand are cheaper than in the States, including the CrossFit membership. I signed up for a monthly unlimited pass - for $87 a month - and promised myself I would go five days a week. I had four months before I would be completely out of money and knew that my best chance at getting in shape before returning home was to work out and dedicate to nothing but.

What I did next would be considered insane back home; however, the ease of moving apartments in Thailand isn't much harder than checking into a different hotel. I decided that since I would be spending the majority of my time doing CrossFit that I should move as close to the gym as possible. So, I moved directly behind it! I needed something cheap and ended up in the worst room I've ever lived in. My monthly rent was only $117 and I was the only non-Thai person living there. I had no kitchen, fridge or even a TV. All my room included was a simple bed and a table. There was a giant construction site in front of my building which was my only view. I didn't realize at the time but I was living below the poverty line but, hey, I was close to the gym.

After my first intro to CrossFit sessions, where we learned the fundamentals, I jumped straight into the regular morning class. I'd wake up, drink a protein shake and walk around the construction site to the gym an half hour early so I could stretch and warm up before class. I loved it and it rekindled my passion for life.

From day one I got to play with giant tires, kettlebells and learned how to properly squat. I loved the short, intense workouts and that we were supposed to write down our times every single day to be compared to everyone else. My favorite moment would be seeing my name and times on the whiteboard at the end of the week, and seeing that I had attended five straight days in a row. Somedays I also started going in the afternoon or to the open gym on Saturdays. On weekends I hung out with the guys I met at the box - I also started calling the gym a "box" -

and began using other CrossFit
terminology: Gym sessions were no longer called workouts, they were
WODs (workout of the days), and we started using terms such as PR to
ask what other members' personal record was for a particular workout.

I had drank the Kool-Aid! My entire wardrobe consisted of nothing but
CrossFit t-shirts, my friends quickly turned into a tribe and, just like a
new member of a cult would do, I started trying to convince everyone I
knew to join their local box.

This dedication - like a drug addiction - was also the catalyst of my
success. That's where Kurt came in. I had told him that I didn't want to
go back to San Francisco because I would miss going to CrossFit. He
looked at me like I was retarded. He said, "You do realize they have
CrossFit all around the world, right?"

It wasn't the fact they didn't have boxes worldwide, though, it was that it
was prohibitively expensive. San Francisco is one of the most expensive
cities in the world and monthly memberships are $250 in the city or $150
if I were to drive across the bridge. There was no way I could afford to
pay that amount or, even if I could, there was no way I could justify
paying that on a gym membership, especially when the gym down the
street from my house only charged $30 a month.

Then Kurt said the one phrase that would sideline my fitness goal and
split it into two. What he said made me realize that being in shape wasn't
enough, and that it was too high up on Maslow's hierarchy of needs to be
my only motivator.

Johnny on the Left and Kurt on the Right at CrossFit Chiang Mai.

"Don't tell yourself you can't afford it. Ask yourself how you can afford it. The solution is simple, stupid, just make $250 more a month." - Kurt M.

It did seem simple - almost too logical. If it wasn't for the millions of questions that suddenly flowed through my head including, how in the world would I make $250 more a month?

Chapter 3: Meeting The Man Who Would Change My Life.

"Our deepest fear is not that we are inadequate. Our deepest fear is that we are powerful beyond measure." - Marianne Williamson

I now had two goals: first, to continue my path to achieving my fitness targets and second, having enough disposable income so I couldn't have any excuses not to. It was time to make my dreams into reality. The only problem was I had no idea where to start.

Fortunately, Kurt forced me to put it down on paper. I wrote down my first goal, "Make more money" which turned out to be a bit too vague. Even though I had heard over and over how important it was to write down and properly define your goals, I never really did or, at least, I would never take it seriously. This time, however, I had to make it work. I still had some doubts but, really, what else did I have to lose? I followed Kurt's formula to properly define my goals and wrote down:

"By July 1st, 2013 I will be making an additional $250 a month in online income through book sales of 12 Weeks in Thailand."

It turns out even that was still a bit too vague to work. The good news, however, is once I had set a realistic goal and end date, I had to start working towards it, consciously or not. I did the only thing I knew how - the one natural talent I was born with - I started meeting people who were smarter than me.

Up until this point, I had been traveling around Thailand for almost four years and had never really met any successful entrepreneurs or, maybe in retrospect, I was never interested in speaking with any of them. But now that I had a goal and a deadline to meet, picking the brains of internet marketers became both my hobby and my passion.

I started listening to the Lifestyle Business Podcast, which has since been renamed the Tropical MBA. I started attending 'Couchsurfing' meet ups and hanging out at coffee shops, hoping to meet people that could teach me something.

Kurt offered to teach me SEO (search engine optimization) but that was never something I was interested in. Getting websites on top of Google results wasn't something tangible in my mind; I wanted to sell a physical product, something real, that people could hold in their hands.

Little did I know I was about to meet a guy from New York that would change my life. The funny thing was, I had already been friends with this guy on Facebook for four years but had never spoken to him even once. We somehow met online after both reading Tim Ferris' 4-Hour Workweek and added each other as friends. He never posted much so I don't even remember seeing any of his updates but, randomly one day, I get a message saying that he would be in town.

 Anton Kraly   4/17, 8:27pm
Hey man,

I'm not sure how we became friends on here (probably through something related to the 4HWW)... but anyway I see that you live in Chiang Mai. I'm going be there next week and I'll be staying in Thailand for a few months.

I was hoping you could give me a recommendation of a good gym to workout at. Not for fighting, just for staying active and getting in good workouts.

I've been thinking about Crossfit Chiang Mai. Are they any good?

Thanks,
Anton

I had asked him if he wanted to meet up for dinner and was expecting a 47 year old man based on his profile photo.

I had just started hanging out with a pilates instructor and I hadn't had sex in months at that point. She asked who I was meeting and asked if she could tag along. I don't know what it was but for the first time in my life I had the power to say no to a beautiful woman and focus on my goals instead. I told her that I had to talk business, even though I really had no idea what the dinner would be like. Attempting to get laid didn't fit my two goals of making more money or getting in shape; if anything, it would have been detrimental to both.

Then he walked in, the man that would make me rich - Anton Kraly.

The first thing I noticed was that, even though he looked like my father's age in his profile photo, he was the same age as me. It would later turn out that he was actually a few years younger. Dinner wasn't that eventful; it was simply professional and informative. I had told him about my book sales on Amazon, and he told me a bit about something he had been successful at called drop shipping which I had previously never heard of.

I wish I could say that I instantly knew it was for me and that was the moment my life changed for the better. But I was stupid or, at least, blind. I was so hung up on selling more books and focusing on generating more book sales that it took me a couple weeks to even sit down and google, "What is drop shipping?", to eventually reading an article on Wikipedia that would give me the basics. Then it hit me. It was a way to sell physical products without having to buy them upfront, store them in a warehouse or ship them yourself to your customers.

You would basically become an authorized dealer for name brand manufacturers and sell their products online. When the customer would buy something from your store, you would collect the money, forward the order to the manufacture and take a cut of the profits. It sounded perfect. The only problem was I had no idea how to get started, so I messaged Anton. He sent me a link to his online training course at AntonMethod.com and wished me the best of luck. I watched the first video and knew I had found something both legitimate as well as doable.

I wish I had jumped straight into building my first store but, in honesty, it took me another three weeks of doing nothing to even get myself to sit down and watch the rest of the videos. I don't know what was holding me back, laziness or simply not seeing the opportunities in front of me. Luckily, a few weeks later, I got another message from Anton saying that he had just spent the past few weeks traveling around the islands and was coming back up to Chiang Mai to settle down for a bit.

I knew I had to finish watching the videos before he arrived so I wouldn't bother him with a bunch of dumb questions that he had already answered. It turns out the entire reason why he recorded the Anton Method videos was because people kept asking him the same questions and he figured it would be easier this way. It worked out well, too, as his very own sister recently used his course to start her own drop shipping business without ever asking him a question, although I'm sure he would have been happy to help.

After watching the videos I started thinking of niches to get into - using the criteria in the course - and a funny thing would happen. Every day around 3:30 I would think of a new, brilliant idea for a niche to get into. I would be tempted to skip CrossFit to stay and do research but, luckily, my first goal was still fitness so I'd force myself to never miss a class. In retrospect, giving my brain a break, increasing my endorphins through the workout and giving myself a night to properly think about the niches, gave me clarity that I normally wouldn't have had. It turns out that mixing business and fitness are really the only ways to become successful.

A guy named JP, who is the CEO of a multi million dollar company once told me that he starts every morning with a workout - no matter what. He mentioned that he's never heard of anyone who is extremely successful in business that doesn't workout or focus on their health. You get a lot of fat, overweight middle managers but C-Level executives are almost always fit or at least value the importance of exercise.

I didn't plan it this way but by focusing first on getting in optimal shape, I would have the energy, mental focus and drive to succeed in business. Even though CrossFit gave me the workout ethics and foundations to get in shape, it was ultimately finding the 'perfect diet' that would help me reach my goals.

Chapter 4: A Diet I Could Stick To

My entire life I had struggled with yo-yo diets and being overweight. Even as a kid I was chubby and it got worse after college when I started working a 9-5 job sat behind a cubicle all day. But I was surprised that, even while traveling, living in Thailand and doing Muay Thai twice a day I could still be fat. I couldn't understand it but accepted it as a reality. I believed I had terrible genetics that would make me gain weight even if I ate the same thing my skinny Asian friends would eat.

I was ready to swear off all diets, especially after unsuccessfully doing Tim Ferris' slow carb diet from the 4-Hour Body. He was my idol. I had done everything he said in his first book, the 4-hour Workweek and it worked perfectly. I used his advice to simplify my life, and moved to Thailand to "retire" by the time I was 28. I even took his chapter about "How to become an expert in any field" to heart and was given the opportunity to be a guest lecturer at Harvard University by following his advice. If the 4-Hour Body diet wouldn't work, I was at a loss as to what would.

For those who aren't familiar with slow carb, it is similar to Paleo with the exception that beans and legumes are allowed. It was almost impossible to find beans in Asia as it's not common to eat, but I tried my best and ate strict when I was back in the U.S. Ultimately it just didn't work for me. I gained weight and was always full of gas. A few years ago I tried a strict Paleo diet, which made complete sense to me, but I felt like crap and was always hungry. I got so sick of eating steak three times a day, was always still hungry and knew it wasn't something I could continue to follow long term. I got headaches, never had energy and eventually gave up on it.

It wasn't until I started doing CrossFit, and being surrounded by others who were following the diet religiously, did I decide to give Paleo another shot. Even though I had been trying to eat Paleo for months up to that point, I realized that I wasn't 100% dedicated. This time, I went all the way and decided to never have cheat days or allow myself any excuses. I stopped drinking alcohol and stopped eating dessert, including fruit, for the time being. I started getting my vitamins from green leafy vegetables instead of sugary mangos and lychees. I started using common sense instead of assuming certain things were healthy.

Another big change came from deciding to spend money on healthy food - no matter the cost. I wrote down another financial goal: I wanted to make $2,000 a month from online income so I could afford both the CrossFit membership as well as being able follow the diet exactly, without being too cheap to order a side of avocado or pay more for grass-fed beef.

It took me buying a $10 cookbook to really understand the diet. Even though I had been following Dave Asprey and the Bulletproof Diet online for over a year now, and had pieced together what the diet consisted of, the short summary in the intro to his cookbook was ultimately what made me really understand the diet as a whole. It also got me to finally try Bulletproof Coffee, which I'm sipping on now as I type this. I firmly believe that a good book and the knowledge it contains is worth a thousand times its cost if you use the knowledge and turn it into action.

My dedication to the Bulletproof diet was born. I stocked my fridge with grass-fed butter, gave up all carbs - with the exception of leafy green vegetables everyday and sweet potatoes once a week - and started drinking coffee with butter and coconut oil in the morning. It sounds insane but it started working. By adding more saturated fat into my diet, I started shedding body fat.

I continued to go to CrossFit five days a week and then, to replenish, started going to buffets with Kurt and Anton every night afterwards. I ate more food than ever but still the fat started melting off. Best of all, the mental fog went away and I started thinking clearer, being more productive and having more energy. I was happier, fitter and thinner.

For breakfast I would have either bacon and eggs or a fatty blended coffee, sometimes both. Lunch would consist of three whole eggs, avocado, coconuts, stir fried chicken with vegetables and topped with bacon. Dinner would almost always be some type of buffet, usually Thai BBQ which consisted of BBQing thin slices of beef, chicken and pork belly over charcoal with some veggies on the side. I loved every meal of every single day. It tasted amazing, I was always full, I got to eat as much butter as I wanted and was still losing body fat. It sounded almost too good to be true.

This 11 lb stick of butter would be consumed by the end of the month

Then someone asked me the dreaded question:

"But what about your cholesterol?"

Chapter 5: Never Take Diet Advice From A Fat Man

Things started going well. I made my first sale through my dropshipping store on July 27th and was on target to reach my goal of $2,000 a month in online income. The weight was melting off and I looked and felt better than ever. I knew I had stumbled onto something that worked and was excited to share everything I had learned with all my friends and family. I thought they would be excited to change and would jump on the opportunity to get in shape, quit the jobs they hated and join me on permanent vacation . They weren't excited. Instead of being happy for me, and jumping on board, they questioned everything.

It became a true test of faith and I almost fell back into the trap of unhappiness. I spent half of my trip trying to teach my friend, Mason, how to follow the diet I was on and start his own drop shipping business but, as soon as I left, he went back to his old ways. I, too, got a bit discouraged and started thinking maybe I should just stay in the U.S., grow up and live a normal life. I had a long stressful argument with my good friends, Mike and Mark, about the diet I was on and both of them teamed up on me until I gave in and agreed that they were right that my diet was just a fluke, even though I felt otherwise. Sadly, I since learned not to talk about my diet to anyone, as it is akin to talking about religion and most people have their minds made up.

I was close to staying and even test drove a second hand V8 Ford Mustang, thinking it would be a good idea to have a car. Thinking back, I don't know why I was even considering moving back to the U.S. as my life was starting to look really good in Thailand. Luckily, I convinced myself to take one final trip to Thailand as I finally had some extra income from my online business and would be able to afford to travel to neighboring countries that I had never been to before. I'm glad I did, as this was the trip where I've met not only the love of my life but also some lifetime friends.

Dr. Shannon Weeks and Dr. Alexis Shields were amongst the first new friends I met while back in Thailand. I had dropped into a Muay Thai class at Team Quest Thailand in Chiang Mai and asked them to dinner afterwards. At the time I just assumed they were another couple on vacation wanting to try out Muay Thai but over dinner I realized how interesting their story was. The couple both worked as Doctors in Portland, Oregon and had recently decided to sell their practice and move to Chiang Mai. Shannon was working on a video training course that taught other doctors Applied Kinesiology. Alexis specialized in Naturopathic Health and Nutrition and makes a living through Skype consults with patients having chronic problems back in the U.S.

It was time to start tracking results and Dr. Shields was the perfect person to do it. She wrote up a list of blood tests to get done, and sat down with me for an entire hour to explain exactly what everything meant and how my current diet was affecting it. I recorded the entire conversation thinking that my two friends back in the U.S., Mike and Mark, would love the answer to our diet debate backed up by an expert with lab results in hand. Neither of them ever even listened to the recording, as far as I know. I realized that even your best friends will hold you back - intentionally or not. I really don't think they had any bad intentions but making me second guess myself, the diet, and research behind something I was having success with does help. If anything I wish they would have said something as simple as, "Well it's clearly working for you, so keep at it". Even your family, who genuinely loves you, won't always be supportive or help you succeed.

I knew that I was at a fragile point in my life and wasn't yet strong enough to defend against criticism and doubt, so I started avoiding all negative people and cutting them out of my life. As much as I love my parents, I even limited the conversations I had with my mom and dad so they wouldn't feed the self doubt. I so badly wanted to succeed but it seemed like everyone else wanted me to stay the same, even if staying the same meant being overweight, stressed out and unhappy. I know friends and family have good intentions, but sometimes it feels like they'd rather see you stay the same even if you are miserable than take any amount of risk to reach for your goals.

On paper everything was going well. My blood tests came back with great results, my blood pressure went down, my cholesterol had good ratios and my bank account started growing along with my new business. The only thing that was going down were the inches around my waist and the pounds on the scale. I knew that whatever I was doing was working and I needed to continue on the path - no matter what anyone else said.

I needed to surround myself with like-minded, positive people and keep away from those who were holding me back but I didn't know where to start.

Chapter 6: Joining A Tribe Of Entrepreneurs

I had stumbled into an underground world of location-independent entrepreneurs. I signed up for a membership at a coworking space here in Chiang Mai and started meeting people from around the world who were all doing the same thing. I could hardly believe it. Every Friday morning we would meet at a member's house to have Paleo breakfast and talk business. They had a cook come in to crack open fresh coconuts, make Bulletproof coffee and scramble up omelettes with avocado. We had an event called the Focus 55, where a group of us would work on our online businesses together for three days in a row, stopping only to sleep and update each other on our progress. It was during these weekend crash course events that I built entire websites and even new businesses. At least once a week we would take over restaurants with reservations for 30 and all openly share what were were doing to make money while traveling the world.

You would think living in a city such as San Francisco, near Silicon Valley, that it would have been easier to meet other entrepreneurs. But, in reality, people in San Francisco are busy trying to come up with the $3,000 that is due for rent at the end of the month. In Chiang Mai it was like college all over again, only this time everyone had money. It was spring break every week. No one had to be at work or in the office if they didn't want to be, and often someone would announce after lunch that they intended to spend the rest of the day at the pool, and everyone would join. We were an army of Bulletproof coffee drinking, Paleo diet eating, online business owners and, best of all, everyone was willing to help each other out.

A daily occurrence, entrepreneurs taking over coffee shops

Anytime I had a question regarding something I couldn't figure out, I would just shout and there would be a programmer or a web developer sitting across who could fix my issue in a minute. I've had people I just met make logos for me, help me with my website and figure out advertising. It was crazy how helpful everyone was, and how much they wanted everyone else to succeed. There was no 'crab in a barrel' mentality like I was used to back in the States, and everyone was always open to new ideas and possibilities. Chiang Mai was the entrepreneurs paradise.

Then, one day, everyone left.

It was the start of burning season, where farmers in the hills burn last year's crops to make room for the next. Although the sky was still perfectly clear and the air crisp and clean, one by one, everyone started leaving in anticipation. My friends started to move to other countries or down to the islands and it started getting lonely once more. Both Anton and Kurt had moved to South America and I was the only one left in

Thailand. I was tempted to follow suit but the idea of a 35 hour plane ride from Asia to South America didn't sound pleasant to me at all. Plus, I had plenty to keep me occupied in Chiang Mai. Although it was a bit lonely going from being surrounded by 20+ people every day, it was a nice break to refocus on what I still needed to accomplish.

"Once in a while it really hits people that they don't have to experience the world in the way they have been told to." – Alan Keightley

But, as spontaneous as it began, we would all somehow meet again like no time had passed at all. This time it would be in Saigon. The funny thing was, I knew nothing about Saigon or even that it was officially known as Ho Chi Minh City, Vietnam. I just knew my friends were there and I finally had the freedom of both time and money to go. This was the first time in my life where I knew I could just pack a bag, grab my laptop and continue my daily life and business from another country without missing a beat or planning a step.

In life there is a conundrum: sometimes you'll have an excess of free time but be broke or at least on a budget, while other times you'll be making a lot of money but always too busy. This was the first time I've ever had both and I knew I had to take advantage of it. I booked a flight and met with Anton in Saigon. The only real plan was to go to coffee shops or maybe check out another co-working space, eat some Vietnamese food and hang out. It was the first time visiting another country where I didn't google any attractions or have a single tourist site on my list of must-sees.

As soon as I landed I was shocked. I didn't know what to expect from Vietnam but suddenly I was out of my element and in a entirely new culture. There were ladies selling coconuts on every street corner, and a Louis Vuitton Store one street away from a street vendor that sold food off the floor. But either way, I was happy to have arrived and to be amongst friends again.

It really hit me at lunch the next day when I suddenly realized that aside from Anton, Alexis and Shannon were both there as well as Kimberly Rich, Mike Gilliand, Euvie Inova, Brandon Nolte, James Ferrer, Lau and Rob Hanly all whom I had met back in Chiang Mai months ago. Everyone I had met had done exactly what I did, we all randomly came to Saigon for no other reason than because everyone else was there. Imagine your entire group of friends from college randomly deciding to move to another country, on a whim, just because they wanted to avoid one month of bad weather...

Aside from seeing everyone I already knew, I also met a ton of other people who were just as interesting. A girl named Kym Pham has an Instagram so popular that hotels will buy her plane tickets and pay for her entire trip just so she can post photos onto her account while she's there. A guy named Ben Hebert had founded the supplement company, Natural Stacks, which just a few months later topped a million dollars in sales. I also got to meet one of my biggest inspirations when I was getting started, Dan Andrews of the Tropical MBA and cofounder of the digital nomad group, the DC.

Saigon was a madhouse and it was there that I became more inspired than ever. The only thing left was figuring out a way to share some of this inspiration with the rest of the world.

Chapter 7: Traveling Like A Boss And Sharing It With Others

I was having breakfast at the 'Paleo house' when a guy named Terry Lin, host of the 'Build My Online Store Podcast' asked if I wanted to be a guest on his show. It came as a surprise to me as, just the week before, I thought he was some sort of a celebrity. Growing up it seemed the only guys that had radio shows were people like Howard Stern, and even Joe Rogan had been on TV before starting his podcast. But it was during that interview with Terry, who was interested in my journey into e-commerce, that I realized how easy it was.

A week later I had started my own podcast and named it, 'Travel Like a Boss Podcast.' My intent was to interview all of the interesting entrepreneurs I met while traveling as I knew how big of an impact meeting guys like Anton and Kurt was for my own success and wanted to share their stories and advice with the world. My criteria was simple: guests had to be successful in whatever location-independent business they had, and they needed to actually travel.

Being back in the U.S. I met a ton of rich and successful people but the problem was, none of them could go on a trip longer than 2 weeks and most of them couldn't even get away for one. I knew that the more people I interviewed and their stories I shared, the more inspired people who were still working jobs they hated back home would be to do it themselves.

Having the show also gave me an excuse to sit down with incredible people and pick their brains for an hour instead of paying them $115 for a consultation.

Just a week after talking to Anton about potential tax loopholes I had the owner of 'Greenback Expat Tax Services' on the podcast. By having him on the show I came to realise that, if I simply stayed out of the U.S. for more than 330 days a year, I could save up to $30,000 in income taxes. It was a no-brainer, especially since my annual cost of living in Chiang Mai is half of that. Saving $30k on taxes would essentially allow me to live for free, and use that extra money to invest into other businesses and travel.

The show also gave me the excuse to sit down with people I was already friends with and really get into some deep conversations about travel, business and the pros and cons of living the digital nomad lifestyle.

I never expected the TLAB Podcast to get as popular as it is today but I'm glad it's out there and am thankful for all of the listeners as well as the guests who come on the show.

A lot of people have asked me why I share so much information out there on the things I'm currently doing when ultimately it leads to more competition. I've been tempted to keep it all a secret - as most people do - but I realized that if I did, I would be thinking too small. I have no idea where this is all going to take me five years from now but I know for sure having an abundance mentality is better than having a scarcity mindset. As far as I'm concerned there is enough money to be made online for everyone to have a piece of the pie. The more people that start traveling and the bigger this entrepreneur community gets the more fun it'll be. The world is a big place and the internet is even bigger.

The best thing is, by publicly announcing my goals to the world, it keeps me accountable. I doubt I would be wearing this gold watch on my wrist right now if I hadn't set the challenge in episode 10 of the podcast.

Chapter 8: A Taste Of Success

Achieving some goals took longer than others while other goals seemed like they were easier than I ever thought possible.

It took me exactly two months to get my first drop shipping store up and running but once the first sale came in I started getting orders everyday. Checking back on my blog, one of the goals I had written down was to generate an income of $1,000 by December 2013 and $2,000 by July 2014 from my dropshipping store. At the time I thought they would be reasonable yet difficult goals to achieve. Since my monthly budget at the time was $600, making double or triple that would allow me to significantly upgrade my lifestyle and have enough excess income to both save and travel.

It turns out that the first month after getting my store up and running, $2k in profits started coming in pretty easily and consistently.

I also had my fitness goals which I realized would take longer to achieve than I had hoped for. When I started I was unhealthy and overweight. In retrospect, I could have sped up the process a bit by dieting harder or working out more often but, this time around, I decided no matter how long it takes, as long as I am making steady progress, I'm happy. I started traveling a lot more often and stopped working out on a set schedule. I kept to the diet even though it was harder while visiting countries such as Cambodia and Vietnam, especially since there were a ton of local foods I wanted to try.

Having a new stream of income was both a blessing as well as a curse.

Being able to finally afford to travel, instead of bootstrapping in one city in Thailand, allowed me to start seeing more of Southeast Asia. The $600 a month budget worked fine when I was living in one place, eating at local places and paying monthly for rent. Traveling, however, instantly increases your monthly spend three-fold as, aside from plane tickets, taxis and not knowing the area, paying nightly at hotels is a lot more expensive than renting a local apartment.

Even though both Cambodia and Vietnam are relatively cheap to travel through, I was never able to afford it until now. I got to see some amazing places: the ancient Angkor Wat temples in Siem Reap, pristine islands down in Koh Rong and the great city of Saigon in Vietnam.

At Angkor Wat in Siem Reap, Cambodia

It was in Vietnam I realized that, even though I had been traveling and spending a lot more money that I normally would have, my income had grown to a point where I had been saving more than I was able to spend.

It's a great feeling knowing that even while you are on vacation your bank account is growing, simply because your passive income out earns your active spending.

Passive Income > Active Spending = Happy Travels.

In December 2013, I randomly mentioned on one of my podcast episodes that one of my goals was to become a Thai Millionaire and have 1,000,000 Thai Baht in my bank account by the end of 2014. I gave myself an entire year to work towards that goal and as a reward for achieving that I was going to buy myself a gold watch.

Growing up in America I always thought that the token of success was graduating from college, getting a good job, working for a company until you were 65 and retiring with a pension. During the retirement ceremony the company would give you a gold watch to thank you for 30 years of service.

I had no idea if my goal would actually be possible but I wanted to have that watch and $30k in the bank. To me, becoming a Thai Millionaire would give me enough savings that I knew I would never have to worry about money again, as I was used to living for less than $1,000 a month and could bootstrap even if something drastic happened and I couldn't work for a year or two. Having that financial buffer would give me plenty of time to start another business and generate a new source of income.

The gold watch would be my symbol of retiring from the workforce, never having to go back to a normal 9-5 job again, never having to hand in another application or go through another job interview, sit through another boring company meeting or be an employee again. When I announced it I didn't sit down to do the math to see how much I would have to save up each month to hit my goal by the end of the year, I just knew I had to continue to make more money while keeping my spending in check.

It was there, in Saigon, a few days after I had paid off all of my credit cards and invoices that I realized I had achieved my goal. I had $29,995 in my bank account, just a few dollars short of reaching my goal, nearly half a year early. I double checked my credit card balances and realized that instead of waiting for another $5, I would just count the money I had in my wallet and celebrate that day. Doing the math almost six months later, I just realized that I suck at math and was way off. Even at a favorable 32:1 exchange rate, a million Thai Baht is actually $31,259 so I was actually over a thousand dollars short. But none of that actually mattered, it was all an arbitrary number anyways. The difference between having $30k or $31.2k in the bank was negligible as both seemed impossible to me at the time anyways.

I still remember the moment I realized I finally had reached my goal, or at least thought I had. It was a Sunday morning and I was having breakfast with Shannon and Anton while watching the UFC fights. I checked my online balances on my phone before fights and couldn't figure out how it was possible. It turns out that, subconsciously, ever since I had decided on the $30k savings goal, I stopped spending money on stupid things and started saving and watching my bank account grow like it was a sport. Instead of doing what most people do - spending more as you start making more - I kept living a similar lifestyle as I did when I was making $1,000 a month even though I was now making a lot more than that.

I had started another drop shipping store in a different niche using the same methods I had originally learned from Anton. The beauty of owning online stores is, unlike trying to get a 10% raise in your salary or working more hours, you can literally double your monthly income by replicating your techniques in a different niche.

Best of all, everything was automated.

I had hired my first employee, a gal named Teresa who lived in South Carolina and spoke with a sweet southern accent. She wasn't the best employee but whenever customers called in to check on their orders, they would feel like they were talking to their grandmother and were always polite and pleasant.

In addition to my drop shipping stores, I had also created the 'Optimize Like a Boss' course which started bringing in sales as well. The concept started completely by accident when Anton overheard me helping another member of his course.

I had been showing him the techniques I used on my own stores to increase conversion rates and sales - and it worked. A few days later the guy who I was helping, Steven, came to me at Punspace, the co-working spot, and told me that he went from making an average of one sale per week to making sales every day since he spoke to me. Anton asked if I could do screen records of everything I taught him, and a few weeks later 'Optimize Like a Boss' was born.

Up until now we've not spent a single dollar marketing it; actually, the only marketing done on it was sending out a single email announcing that it was now available. We just figured that if the content was good, and the initial people who bought it started seeing more sales, they would tell others and word would slowly spread. It worked. It was the most counterintuitive internet marketing launch ever and, even if you've listened to all of my podcasts and read my blog from day one, you might not have even known it was available until now.

As of writing this, we're selling quite a few OLAB memberships and sales continue to grow. It's been a nice supplemental part of my income although it's still a tiny fraction of what I make compared to my actual drop shipping stores.

How much money was I making at this point? I honestly have no idea. All I knew was I was saving money faster than I could spend it and, suddenly, I woke up with $30k in the bank. The best thing about it was, less than a year ago I was down to my last $200 with no real plan or hope for the future. I had even considered moving back in with my parents and getting a normal job. Thinking about it now doesn't even make sense. How could I have ever been so desperate to even consider moving back in with my parents? I'm glad it never got to that point, as I know I would have went crazy living under my parents' roof as an adult, even if it was only temporary.

Walking to the mall that afternoon I was hoping they would have the exact watch I had been having my eye on. One of my favorite hobbies for the past few months had been window shopping for gold watches. It turns out that gold hasn't been in style since the 90's, so most places had a limited selection. I figured that a reasonable amount to spend would be a few thousands dollars so I looked at watches by Tag Heuer, Cartier and even some entry level Rolex watches. Spending $5,000 out of the $30k I had saved up didn't seem like a big deal, especially since it was something that I would cherish forever. But as luck would have it, the one watch I really liked was a moderately priced watch made by Citizen. I've had my eye on it now for the past couple of months and was excited to see that they had it in Saigon.

The funny thing was, since the watch wasn't actually that expensive, I could have just bought it without worrying too much about the price months ago; however, since I had a goal to hit, I forced myself to wait.

"Patience is power. Patience is not an absence of action; rather it is "timing" it waits on the right time to act, for the right principles and in the right way." — Fulton J. Sheen

Trust me when I tell you it was worth the wait. Every time I look down at that shiny gold watch even today, it reminds me of where I came from and what it took to become successful. It truly became a symbol of my achievements but, more importantly, it's a symbol of freedom. Knowing that I've now developed the knowledge and skills to run my own business and never have to work for another boss again. The gold watch is my mental insurance that I am now retired from the corporate world, and will never again, for the rest of my life need to apply for another job or answer to another boss ever again.

The mission now is to help and encourage others to take the Gold Watch challenge and create an army of successful digital entrepreneurs worldwide.

At the Citizen Shop in Saigon

Chapter 9: Taking The Gold Watch Challenge

I firmly believe that by simply setting a challenge for myself started the momentum to make it happen. All I did was: figure out a somewhat attainable goal, a timeline of when I wanted it done by, and then announced it to the world. If you currently have $0 in your bank shooting for $10k might be a good starting point. If you already have $30k then shoot for $50k. By simply setting a new goal, you'll subconsciously work towards it every single day.

Instead of itching to go out and buy the latest iPhone, new clothes or celebrating every weekend with drinks at the bar, your new favorite hobby will be watching your bank account grow. The best thing is, once you hit one goal, it's easy to set another.

My new goal? Become a Vietnamese Billionaire by the end of the year. There I said it. I set the goal, made a timeline and announced it to the world. How much is a Billion Vietnamese Dong in U.S. Dollars? Currently around $47k, but we'll shoot for an even $50k just to give it a nice round number. How am I going to do that? I'll leave it up to fate.

Knowing that I have that goal up in the air, everything I do will now be calculated with that in mind. It'll force me to work harder on my drop shipping stores, spend less on frivolous things and inspire me to create new businesses. Keep setting higher and higher goals.

What you get by achieving your goals is not as important as what you become by achieving your goals. -- Henry David Thoreau

#GoldWatchChallenge

I'm so inspired right now that I just randomly decided something crazy. If you accept the challenge and save up $30k this year, I am going to buy the watch with my own money and give it to you as a gift.

The funny thing is, once you actually reach the goal, spending a couple of hundred dollars or even a few thousand dollars on a gold watch won't matter to your bank account, but knowing that you went from reading this book, setting a goal and having the author give you a Gold Watch for completing your goal is priceless.

So here it is and here are the rules. If you want to accept the challenge, write down your goal, and let it be known to the world. Do one or all of these things, the more you make it known, the more likely you will reach your goals. For me I announced it on my podcast.

Don't have one yet?

Tweet it at me @johnnyfdk #goldwatchchallenge and I'll start following you.

Make a blog post announcing that you are accepting the challenge and link it to me. Or even just write on my facebook wall that you are joining the challenge.

My goal is to have an army of entrepreneurs wearing Gold Watches. Join the army and accept the challenge.

"Don't believe me, just watch." - *Tyga*

Chapter 10: The Tables Have Turned

"Sex is like air, it's not a big deal unless you're not getting any."

It had been eight months since I dated, had sex or even went out to a bar. I had decided that my priority was to get in shape and to build a successful business. For the first time in my adult life, I had swore off women completely. To be honest, this could have been the most vital part of achieving success in reaching my fitness and financial goals even though at the time it didn't feel that way nor was it the intention.

Most men never think about it but a majority of our time and energy involves meeting, dating, texting or chasing women. The quest started as a teenager and never stopped until now. I had promised myself that, until I reached both my fitness and financial goals, I would stay away from women. It was actually easier than I thought. I stopped completely and went cold turkey. No texting, no bars, no clubs, no dates, and no porn - nothing. And then something magical happened; all of a sudden I had seemingly unlimited focus and mental clarity. To some men it would be devastating but losing my sex drive was the best thing that ever happened to me. It felt like I had an extra 8 hours in the day and since I was no longer trying to impress the opposite sex, I actually had the time and energy to work on things to impress myself. I didn't allow myself to turn into a slob or anything so I still maintained good hygiene, wore clean clothes and seemed like a well-adjusted, normal guy from the outside. I'd hang out with the boys and would simply skip the going out to the bar portion of our days. My friends thought I was crazy but it worked.

One day, 8 months later, I woke up and realized my drop shipping stores were doing well and I was in the best shape of my life thanks to my focused diet and workout routine. My natural testosterone had skyrocketed from being healthy and back in shape. It was time to start dating again but I had no idea where to start.

I hadn't touched alcohol in months and decided that the health benefit of being sober wasn't something I was willing to give up just to get laid. I didn't want to sacrifice the months of hard work, and the gains in my health, just to have drinks with a girl with the possibility of getting lucky. If I was going to hook up it would have to be on my terms.

I was rusty and didn't actually know what to do anymore, so I started going out everyday and basically announced to the world I was ready to date again. This time, though, something was different. After the initial few days of awkwardness I realized that I was more confident than ever. I was in great shape, had enough money not to worry about who was going to pay the bill and, most importantly, I was proud of my new businesses and spoke with passion and enthusiasm about everything going on in my life.

Katherina, a pretty girl from Switzerland, was the first to notice. We started hanging out regularly but since she was only in town for a couple months we both decided to keep it casual. Then out of nowhere came a girl from Australia, then one from France and then another from Finland. My dating life went from zero to a full plate within a matter of a couple of weeks. Never in my adult life had I experienced anything like it. No amount of chat up lines, routines or gimmicks I've read in books or saw in movies even came close. For once in my life, women were chasing me instead of the other way around.

I had finally figured out the key to success with women. It was actually right in front of my eyes the entire time. I'm sure most guys know it as well but just don't want to admit it. Attractive women are attracted to attractive men. But instead of spending our time becoming attractive by eating healthy, going to the gym and developing ourselves, most men spend it trying to get girls drunk, learning pick up lines, and finding tips and tricks.

I had just spent the past 8 months doing the opposite as most men do. I was working on myself and not worrying about what women thought. I was genuinely proud of myself, my accomplishments, physique, business and my future. For once in my life it wasn't 'fake it until you make it', bragging or having a big ego, it was an unspoken quiet confidence that showed every time I smiled. I was suddenly always full of energy and always in a great mood.

Every woman is universally attracted to confident, in shape, successful men and I, somehow, became that man.

"The rich get richer, the poor get poorer. Success breeds success, and desperation reeks of desperation."

I was happy, healthy and optimistic about life, my work, places I wanted to travel to, the places I've been. I had enough choice where I knew I didn't have to be desperate. I was in the position to become that suave player my teenage self dreamed about being, dating multiple women and hooking up every other night. I finally had the chance to become that guy every teenage boy dreams of becoming.

But, then, something happened. Someone happened. Someone completely unexpected came into my life and a single kiss made me instantly forget about everyone else.

Chapter 11: Falling in Love

Her name was Larissa and she was the girl who would complete my life.

We'd met at the most beautiful festival on the face of the planet a month prior but never exchanged details or much more than just a pleasant conversation. Every year in Thailand, there is a lantern festival where monks chant for hours and the skies fill with paper lanterns fueled by candlelight. I'd love to say it was a night of romance and that we both lit our lanterns at the same time, caught each other's eyes from across the field and, from thousands of paper lanterns floating through the air, ours found each other and entwined as they soared up to the heavens together.

But the truth is we met in front of the restrooms after a grueling hour of walking through the crowds to find our bus ride home! Her friend, Donna, had walked into the unisex bathroom where I was standing at the urinal and we had a bit of a laugh about it thinking she was in the wrong bathroom. I had a quick chat with Larissa having no idea that she had seen me in the crowd earlier that evening and found me attractive. We didn't exchange phone numbers, last names or even asked each other if we were just in town for vacation or living there. I honestly didn't think I'd ever see her again and thought of it as just a nice chat. It turns out that fate would think differently. The western expat community in Chiang Mai is relatively small and, a few weeks later, Larissa found me through a friend of a friend.

We met one night for drinks at a local Thai bar called the Maldives, which is themed like Sea World back in the States without the animal cruelty. A bit cheesy of a venue but I knew they had live music and would be a quiet place to talk and hang out. I sipped on a club soda and Larissa had one drink. I honestly had no idea what or who to expect, but suddenly I had to leave in a rush halfway through our first date. I was so enthralled by Larissa that I realized I had foolishly left the keys in the ignition of my newly rented motorbike 6 blocks away. I must have been nervous and I had the right to be. Larissa was beautiful; she appeared out of nowhere into my life. She caught me completely off guard.

I ran almost a kilometer to grab the keys out of my rental bike that was sitting in front of a busy 7-Eleven where we had met. I was both surprised and grateful that no one had driven off with it. When I returned I convinced Larissa to sit next to me so we could watch the band play but, secretly, I just wanted to sit closer to her. It was pleasant but it wasn't until the end of the night that I realized she was the one, I doubt she knew it at the time but I had already decided that I wanted to see a lot more of her.

It was when I had walked her to her bike and kissed her goodnight that I realized how perfect we were for each other. I've kissed a lot of girls in my life but that first kiss in front of Maldives is one I will never forget. I instantly knew we had chemistry like I've never seen before - I had to be with her. She was the one and she made me forget about every other girl I was seeing. I doubt she knows I was already seeing other people before we met but I'm glad it worked out that way. It proves to myself that I chose her because she was the one I wanted and not because she just happened to be there. She was the perfect girl for me and still continues to be so.

It's been over six months since we first kissed and I still smile every time I think about that moment, as well as about her. The first couple of months was difficult. I wasn't used to being a couple, as it had been so long since I had been in a relationship. But we made it work. My initial plan was for us to never fight or argue. The first time we did, I freaked out thinking that it was over.

'Well that was great while it lasted.' I thought. Silly me, I didn't even realize that it's normal for couples to fight. Couples work things out and, if anything, we became 10x stronger every time we did.

I'd like to think that we would have ended up together regardless if I was in shape or successful but, the reality is, everything happens for a reason and maybe it was fate's intention to have us meet when we did. A year ago I wouldn't have been ready for a relationship but now I'm happy that she came into my life. Meeting Larissa was truly the blessing on top of everything else that had been going so well in my life. Ever since that first day just 8 months ago when I decided to start setting big goals and to work towards achieving them no matter the sacrifice.

By the way, Larissa doesn't know this but, even though I've dated a lot of people in the past, she's the first and only girl that has ever heard me say the words, "I love you". I told her that one day she would find out she means more to me than she knows and this is the reason why.

Falling in love wasn't a goal that I set or wrote down but it was a goal that truly completed the trifecta of happiness. Being in great shape, having a successful business and a loving relationship is everything that I could ever ask for. I've never been this happy. Now my goal is to help others achieve the same level of success and happiness in their own lives. The trifecta of happiness is a gift I want everyone reading this book to experience as well.

The rest of the book is going to be dedicated to helping you achieve it for yourself. I already have everything I've ever dreamed of and couldn't possibly be happier. Now it's your turn.

The only thing I could think of to make my life even better is sharing it with others.

"Love only grows by sharing. You can only have more for yourself by giving it away to others." — *Brian Tracy*

Chapter 12: The Seven Steps To Success.

I'd love to say that there is a universal path to success but I don't know if there is. It took me 32 years to figure out my path but, hopefully, by sharing it with you it'll save you some of the headache and time I've already spent.

I'll go more into each step in detail throughout the book but here is a summary of each and how it helped me.

Step 1: De-stress Your Life.

I contribute a huge part of my success with having the free time to dedicate to self improvement. The first step I took was decluttering my life. I got rid of everything I didn't need and freed up my time, energy and resources to work towards building a better life. If you haven't already, read my first book at 12WeeksinThailand.com for details on how I quit my job and moved to Thailand - even with no savings.

Also read the 4-Hour Workweek by Tim Ferris, and follow the elimination chapter, which had a huge impact on my life.

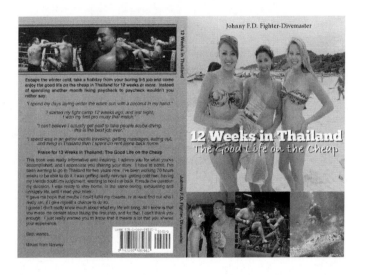

Step 2: Get Healthy, Get In Shape.

I truly believe that being healthy, eating clean and being lean has given me the energy, mental clarity and focus to achieve my other goals. Work on this while you declutter, and continue working on it, as it is the longest process. The good news, however, is that once you're in shape it is a million times easier to maintain it. I personally follow the Bulletproof Diet by Dave Asprey and recomend getting started with a Paleo type diet by following Mark Sisson's 21 day Primal Blueprint challenge.

As for fitness, I started with CrossFit but would recommend finding a good trainer who teaches you great form. I also highly recommend the Stronglifts 5x5 workout as an alternative to CrossFit.

Step 3: Set Specific Goals.

The next step was writing down and clearly defining my goals. Starting with just one goal at a time and dedicating my all towards it, they have since become a reality for me. Write down specific goals, when you plan to achieve each one and, more importantly, how you plan on achieving each goal.

Go to my blog JohnnyFD.com and download my free 5 Steps to Freedom video by signing up for my newsletter to get started setting your own goals.

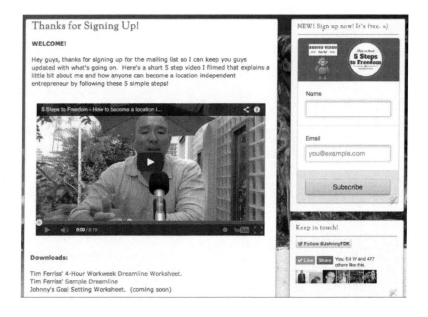

Step 4: Become Your Own Boss.

Even though it's possible to have a location-independent job while still working for someone else, I truly think the goal should be to be in charge of your own destiny and income. Instead of spending the hours of your day working and making money for someone else, why not do it for yourself and build your own legacy?

"There's always a sucker in the room and if you don't know who it is, it's normally you."

Either you are working extremely hard and making your boss a ton of cash (instead of making it for yourself) or you are selling yourself short by being lazy. You may think you are getting ahead by doing the least amount of work possible and still getting paid for it but trust me, at the end of the day, you're just wasting your own time. You are the sucker in the room for wasting everyone's damn time. Everyone will have their own path to starting a business but if you want to follow the same path I took you can start here. (johnnyfd.com)

If you want to read the full 5 year story about how I made enough money to finally fund my travels you can read the entire blog post here: The Full Story. (johnnyfd.com) It wasn't easy by the way; it took me 4 years to figure out that blogging was never going to replace my income, and neither would writing books. I looked into freelancing and working for others, working as a teacher or a guide wherever I went but, ultimately, it was starting my own business that finally paid off. But even then it wasn't easy, it still took months of hard work and dedication before I made my first sale.

Step 5: Stay Motivated, Motivate Others.

By having a public blog and a podcast, it makes it extremely easy to stay motivated. If a week passes and I'm not doing well in business or making progress, it's embarrassing for me. Make yourself accountable and help others along the way. The best way to keep ahead of the game is to teach it, this forces you to constantly review the basics.

Help others who are just starting out, by sharing your experience, creating a group, blog, podcast, or any other means to force yourself to stay ahead of the curve. Ever since I've started my blog and podcast I've forced myself to stay in shape, to take time off to travel and to continue to build my business to be more and more successful. You can do the same.

Some of my favorite guests have been people who have taught me something that motivated me right away. Sabrina from episode 41 (travellikeabosspodcast.com) who makes $3,000 a month from her blog Just One Way Ticket, taught me how to change my style of blogging from random one-off articles, into comprehensive evergreen articles that people will actually share and go back to months or even years later.

I also learned a ton from interviewing guests such as Ryan Daniel Moran, Dr. Alyssa Marshall, Mark Brenwall, Ben Hebert, Alan Vantoai and others.

Step 6: Don't Look For Love, Welcome It.

I used to think that I'd be lucky if I met a nice girl that wanted to be with me. Now that I've been in a great relationship, I've realized that it's not luck. When you have your life together, love comes to complete it. When your life is a mess and you are looking for love to complete you, love will hide; however, as soon as you don't need anyone else to fulfill you, doors open and all you have to do is walk through.

Confidence is earned, not learned. For every hour you would have spent looking for love or figuring out ways to make yourself seem attractive, you could have actually spent it becoming more attractive. People often forget that the root word of attractive is attract. Work on yourself first and you will naturally attract others into your life.

at·tract
/əˈtrakt/ ◀))

verb

cause to come to a place or participate in a venture by offering something of interest, favorable conditions, or opportunities.
"a campaign to attract more visitors to West Virginia"

- evoke (a specified reaction).
"I did not want to attract attention"

- cause (someone) to have a liking for or interest in something.
"I was attracted to the idea of working for a ballet company"
synonyms: entice, allure, lure, tempt, charm, win over, woo, engage, enthrall, enchant, entrance, captivate, beguile, bewitch, seduce
"he was attracted by her smile"

"Love yourself first and everything else falls into line. You really have to love yourself to get anything done in this world."

- Lucille Ball

Step 7: Enjoy Life, Don't Sabotage Your Success.

As soon as I started making money I started looking for ways to spend it. First came the gold watch and the window shopping, then came the investment ideas. Either way, it felt like the money was burning a hole in my pocket and I needed to unload it. Luckily, I spent my $20k in Facebook stock and it happens to be doing well. It doesn't seem logical (and it isn't) but as soon as you start becoming successful you'll look for a way to destroy it all - don't!

The first book that really changed my outlook on money was Rich Dad, Poor Dad by Robert Kiyosaki. Another book that was a bit slow and tedious but really shifts your way of thinking about money is The Millionaire Fastlane by MJ DeMarco. Both are great books to read if you still think owning a house is an asset or if you think the term down payment is an option.

I know it's a bit strange to put these '7 Steps To Success' in the middle of the book. Some of the topics I've already talked about, some I will go into throughout the rest of the book, but the reason why it's in here is because I want everyone reading this to take action sooner than later. The steps work; all you have to do is put one foot in front of the other and start walking towards your goals.

Check out my recommended resources page on my blog (johnnyfd.com) as I often update and add to things I currently use that have helped make me successful in health, business, and productivity.

Chapter 13: The Butter Diet

I normally don't like talking about my diet. To me, it's on par with discussing religion. There is so much information out there that everyone thinks they are an expert. But, in reality, no one really knows anything and everything is contradictory. A lot of people have just given up. One day you are told that cholesterol is bad and to avoid saturated fat, use vegetable oil and margarine instead. Then you find out that margarine causes both heart disease and cancer. Instead of blaming margarine the blame is put on Trans fat. Now that it's removed margarine is supposedly good for you again.

It drives me crazy hearing people defend margarine still and putting the blame on Trans fat when the blame should be on whoever convinced you to switch from butter in the first place. Imagine if the same had happened with the locks on your front door. Everything worked perfectly and has been for 200 years. Then one day the media convinces everyone that locks are no longer safe and that everyone should switch to 'lock-grine' devices. Then someone breaks into your house. Not just your house, but across the U.S. break-ins increase by 200x. It turns out that there was something in the lock-grine devices called Trans-lock that instead of preventing people from breaking in, actually makes it easier for people to break in your house. The largest lock manufacturer announces that they will no longer use Trans-lock in their lock-grine! Trans-lock is bad! Our locks are now 100% Trans-lock free!

In that scenario (after getting your house broken into) who would you blame for your house getting broken into? I know I would be pissed at the lock company for convincing me to switch from my perfectly good standard locks to their new ones, which did the exact opposite of what it was designed to do. I wouldn't care if the new locks were Trans-lock free. I would be so angry that I would never again listen to scare tactics on the news. But what happened with margarine and Trans fat was the complete opposite. The majority of the world still avoid butter and opt for "healthy" vegetable oils and whole grains, which also snuck their campaign into there as well.

When it comes to diet and nutrition everyone is confused. It doesn't help that McDonald's now sponsors nutritionist conferences - like the California Dietetic Association - and Doctors averaged only 19.6 hours of nutrition training throughout their 4 years of medical school. Even i've personally spent more than nineteen and a half hours researching proper nutrition and I am far from an expert. There is so much health information out there that is influenced by big business and profits of companies like Monsanto.

The only thing I can promise you for sure is that information regarding nutrition will continue to change, everything is contradictory and that the world is confused. However, I have a solution for you.

The solution is to listen to common sense, especially your own. Eat real food and get health tests to monitor your results. I promise that this simple solution will be better for you in the long run than any book, diet, or expert (including most doctors) can tell you. At the end of the day, you are accountable for your own health and what you put in your mouth and your body.

For me what helped the most was eliminating things that were clearly bad for me - such as sugar and alcohol - then replacing things that had no real nutritional benefit with things that did. I substituted both simple and complex carbs such as rice, wheat and grains with more vegetables. I replaced fruit products including juice, jam, desserts and treats with fresh local fruit that was actually in season. I replaced ice cream, sweets and treats with high quality 91% Dark Chocolate. I replaced standard factory farmed meat with wild or pasture raised meat. I also replaced all of the cheap oil and fat in my diet with more expensive, higher quality fats such as avocado, extra virgin coconut oil, and butter from grass-fed cows.

It was pretty simple now that I think about it. Eliminate what is clearly bad for you, and replace what may be suspect with the higher quality equivalent - even if it costs more. Since I decided to eat this way my grocery bills have doubled. Instead of spending $2.99 on a dozen eggs, I spend $6 for eggs from a local farm. Instead of spending $2.99 on ground beef, I now spend $7.99 on grass-fed beef. Organic vegetables and fruits are double, and grass-fed butter from Ireland or New Zealand costs three times as much as margarine. The Pink Himalayan sea salt I use costs 10x the price of a 39 cent package of table salt. But here's the thing: everything now tastes better, so I eat less of it, and by doubling my grocery bill I have tripled my income. I'll explain more of that in the next chapter.

"Good food isn't necessarily expensive, bad food is just artificially cheap."

So what do I actually eat? It changes as I travel a lot, but no longer do I let that be an excuse. Even if I have to plan ahead, skip a meal or pay double the price to get good food, that's what I do.

For breakfast I usually have Bulletproof coffee which will both shock and amaze you once you hear what's in it. On weekends I have eggs scrambled in butter, bacon and avocado often with a fresh coconut.

For lunch I normally go out for Thai food or the local cuisine of whatever country I happen to be in. But instead of getting a pad thai or fried rice, I order a stir fry with no rice, and a vegetable or curry dish. My favorites are stir fried mixed vegetables, and a red coconut curry chicken dish without rice.

For dinner I often go to buffets where I can load up on salads and grilled meat or I have a grass-fed steak with a triple serving of vegetables instead of potatoes and bread. My favorite nighttime Thai dish is called Tom Ka Gai which means Coconut Chicken soup.

These are some of my favorite recipes.

Tom Ka Gai: (Chicken Coconut Soup)
I normally order this at restaurants instead of making it myself.

3/4 pound boneless, skinless chicken meat
3 tablespoons coconut oil or grass fed butter
2 (14 ounce) cans coconut milk
2 cups water
2 tablespoons minced fresh ginger root
4 tablespoons fish sauce
1/4 cup fresh lime juice
1/4 teaspoon cayenne pepper
1/2 teaspoon ground turmeric
2 tablespoons thinly sliced green onion
1 tablespoon chopped fresh cilantro

Bulletproof Coffee: (courtesy of Dave Asprey)
I have this monday-friday mornings instead of breakfast.

1.5 Cups of high quality Organic Coffee (Example: Upgraded Coffee)
⅓ of a stick of Grass-Fed Unsalted Butter (Kerrygold or Anchor)
1 Capful of MCT Oil (Upgraded MCT)
Blend together until foamy and drink hot.

Optional:
You can also add Vanilla, Cacao or Cinnamon to taste.

Note:
When you first start drinking Bulletproof coffee, you have to take it slow.
Start with a teaspoon of butter and ½ teaspoon of oil for the first couple
of days until you get your stomach used to it.

Dark Chocolate Covered Macadamia Nuts:
This has become my go-to dessert if I want something sweet.

Lightly coat a tupperware container with coconut oil. (to prevent sticking)
Cover the bottom with crushed macadamia nuts.
Gently melt 2 bars of 85% Dark Chocolate in a pan.
Pour into the container over nuts, refrigerate to set.

I first heard of this weird butter diet at my friend Alexis' birthday party in

San Francisco. Everyone at the party was putting butter in their coffee and dipping vegetable sticks in butter which I found strange; however, everyone was in much better shape than me and had more energy, so I figured they were doing something right. Then Dave showed up to the party! It was this chance encounter on my last day in San Francisco before heading back to Thailand that sparked my new way of eating.

Taken November 2011 when I first met Dave Asprey, the Bulletproof Executive.

Taken a year later after starting the Bulletproof diet. 30lbs lighter.

As far as the diet is concerned, I'm pretty sure I've found the diet I'm going to stick to for the rest of my life. I've heard of and tried countless other diets out there and I've never been able to stick to one for more than a couple of months. But I've been able to stick to the Paleo style of eating and the Bulletproof diet now for more than a year and don't see why I would ever stop eating this way. I enjoy the food, I'm losing body fat, toning muscle, and my health tests keep improving every six months that I've taken them.

I've completely stopped taking all supplements and protein powders, and just started eating real food. Once a week I enjoy eating sweet potatoes or white rice but other times I just drink a lot of water, eat a lot of vegetables cooked in butter, coconuts, avocado and eggs, and grass-fed meat whenever I can find it. When I feel like something sweet I reach for homemade chocolate covered macadamia nuts or just have some high quality black coffee. That's it. It sounds simple - and it really is!

Another good thing about the new way of eating is that I'm never hungry. My body has trained itself to burn stored fat for fuel, which is why the pounds keep shedding off. Instead of eating 6 meals a day I hardly ever eat more than three now. I used to get headaches and lightheadedness whenever my blood sugar dropped from not eating, but I haven't felt like that since I changed my eating habits.

But that's not even the best part!

I'm now more clear-headed and energetic than I've ever been in my entire life. I can't remember a time in my life where I wasn't tempted to take an afternoon nap, especially after a big meal. Now I get excited to explore, seek out new adventures and even go to work. I highly recommend to anyone that wants the most optimal life to focus on improving their diet. If I had to choose the single biggest factor to my newfound happiness today, it would be finally getting in shape and having the energy, confidence and clarity to get things done.

I highly recommend reading The Bulletproof Diet Book by Dave Asprey.

Chapter 14: What about Exercise?

A year ago I was Crossfit obsessed. I went to do 'Workout of the Days' five (sometimes six) days a week. I pushed my body hard to the extremes and got the best workouts of my life - and it worked. I was in great shape but it wasn't sustainable; I knew it wasn't something I could do long term.

Going to Crossfit everyday was a great kick in the pants to start my fitness journey and get me motivated to work on my business. I set and reached my goal of making $250 a month more in passive income so I could afford the high membership wherever in the world I was; however, now I'm taking a bit of a break from the high intensity workouts. Instead I've been following the Mark Sisson protocol which is: move a lot, lift heavy things and sprint.

I have a timer set on my computer which alerts me every half an hour and locks my screen. First off, it makes me a lot more productive as it reminds me to get back to the task at hand instead of browsing Facebook. More importantly, though, it forces me to get up and take a stretch break. I've been alternating between walking barefoot outside onto the grass to get some sun and do a light stretch, and doing William Lee's OfficeFit Workout of pushups and air squats every half an hour. Either way, my eyes are less strained, I focus more throughout the day and my productivity has jumped through the roof.

I used similar tactics when writing my first book, 12 Weeks in Thailand. I had a PC back then so I used the free Window's program, WorkRave. Now that I'm on a Mac, I use Time Out. Either way, by compartmentalizing your day into 30 minute sections you suddenly have 16+ time blocks where you can be extremely productive.

Here is an example of my typical work day.

Block 1: 7:00am-7:30am. Bulletproof Coffee ritual.
1 minute break: 10 pushups and 10 air squats.

Block 2: 7:30am-8:00am. Forward drop shipping store orders.
1 minute break: 10 pushups and 10 air squats.

Block 3: 8:00am-8:30am. Respond to Emails.
1 minute break: 10 pushups and 10 air squats.

Block 4: 8:30am-9:00am. Plan for the day, starting with the hardest thing first.
1 minute break: 10 pushups and 10 air squats.

Block 5: 9:30am-10:00am. Write a chapter in the book.
1 minute break: 10 pushups and 10 air squats.

Block 6: 10:00am-10:30am. Continue writing.
1 minute break: 10 pushups and 10 air squats.

Block 7: 10:30am-11:00am. Add products to my drop ship stores or rewrite descriptions.
1 minute break: 10 pushups and 10 air squats.

Block 8: 11:00am-11:30am. Check Facebook, Twitter, my blogs.
1 minute break: 10 pushups and 10 air squats.

Block 9: 11:30am-12:00pm. Check Member Forums and respond to questions.
1 minute break: 10 pushups and 10 air squats.

Lunch: 12:00pm-1:00pm. Walk to lunch, get 20 minutes of sun. No computers.

Block 10: 1:00pm-1:30pm. Enjoy a coconut while surfing Facebook.
1 minute break: Stretch Break.

Block 11: 1:30pm-2:00pm. Write a blog post.
1 minute break: Stretch Break.

Block 12: 2:00pm-2:30pm. Record a Podcast or continue to blog.
1 minute break: 10 pushups and 10 air squats.

Block 13: 2:30pm-3:00pm. Continue block 12.
1 minute break: 10 pushups and 10 air squats.

Block 14: 3:00pm-3:30pm. Watch funny videos on Youtube, post on Facebook.
1 minute break: 10 pushups and 10 air squats.

Block 15: 3:30pm-4:00pm. Realize I've been messing around all afternoon and start doing the important tasks on my daily to do list.
1 minute break: 10 pushups and 10 air squats.

Block 16: 4:00pm-4:30pm. Rush to finish up the important tasks of the day!

Work Day is Finished: Meet my girlfriend and walk either to the gym, to the pool or to the grocery store. The perfect time to unwind and catch up on each other's days. Workout, shower, go for dinner and/or meet friends. Don't open computer for the rest of the day.

What about Exercise?

My current workout strategy is using my 1 minute breaks to do a very simple quick workout. I got a lot of funny looks the first day but now people are so used to me getting out of my desk every 30 minutes and doing pushups and air squats in the middle of the coworking space that they either ignore it entirely or often join in. I've since then started doing them outdoors as it's nice to get some fresh air as well as get out of everyone's way. By the end of the day I've done over 100 pushups and air squats. You can change them up by doing lunges instead, pullups if you have a bar, or variations of pushups if needed. The basic rule is, once it starts getting easy, make it harder by doing them slower, deeper, with better form or with weights.

The most important thing is moving - often.

On the weekends I frequently go rock climbing, hiking or do something else fun and active, usually outdoors.

I don't need a standup desk or a treadmill desk as I never sit for more than half an hour at a time anyways. The actual gym sessions? They are pretty much optional. If you did my exact mini break routine every day, and you did one Tabatha (20 seconds of ultra-intense exercise followed by 10 seconds of rest, repeated continuously for 4 minutes (8 cycles total) or a sprint session once a week, you would be in great shape. The only reason I even go to the gym is because it's a great way to unwind, clear my head, and it's a nice way to spend time with my girlfriend.

I've also started doing heavier weights at the gym implementing the Stronglifts 5x5 regimen recently. On days I do the program, I still take 1 minute breaks but more to just stretch out and get some fresh air than to actually do an OfficeFit workout. If you want to really get in great shape, I would recommend doing Stronglifts Mondays, Wednesdays and Fridays, and some type of Sprint or Tabata once a week. Just remember it is extremely important to do the lifts with great form so invest in a personal trainer to learn how to properly squat, deadlift, press and row before you start. A big thank you to Ben Finnigan for showing both Larissa and myself proper form during our first few months of the program.

You can download the free Stronglifts app on your iPhone or go to Stronglifts.com for more information. If you're interested in CrossFit I would highly recommend starting with a foundations or intro class and find a trainer who focuses on proper form over heavy weights and personal records.

Taking selfies at the gym are optional.

Living the 4-Hour Workweek and the 4-Hour Body:

You might be thinking, what the heck happened to working only four hours a day? Judging by my example schedule, I wake up at 6:30am, work 8 hours a day, and go to the gym 6 days a week. That sounds like the exact opposite of living the 4-hour workweek. You might be annoyed that the dream was to work as little as possible, hack the exercise portion and never have to step foot into the gym, and here I'm telling you I work more than you most likely do now in your normal life.

But here's the secret:

Both Tim Ferriss and I don't need to work more than four hours a week anymore. But now that we don't have to, we enjoy it and actually want to do it. The thought of having to be at work at a certain time to report to a boss is torture. Being forced to work out 5 days a week as I did when I lived at the Muay Thai camp and was sponsored by the gym was terrible. I hated being forced to wake up early and adhering to a schedule - their schedule. What I didn't tell you is that the above is my typical workday but it is 100% by choice. The other thing I didn't mention is that anytime something better comes up, I take it.

Last Wednesday, for example, I got an offer to go Ziplining in the jungle but it would be from 8:30am-4:00pm, right smack in the middle of the workday. Without hesitation, I went.

I also tend to take the day off whenever someone suggests to go hang out by the pool all afternoon, or on days my girlfriend has a day off. The nice thing about having a location-independent business is you can take a day off whenever you want without having to explain to anyone why you're doing it.

Once a week I just don't feel like working, so instead of forcing myself to stay at the office until 4pm, knowing that I will be unproductive anyways, I simply leave, go home and watch 'Game of Thrones'. Other days I go and get a foot massage while listening to podcasts, which is my other favorite thing to do.

As for working out, I went back to the U.S. for three weeks and didn't go to the gym once. I still did a few active things that I enjoyed, such as indoor rock climbing, but mostly I just kept to the diet and everything was fine. Before my lifestyle and diet change, I would balloon up and gain 20lbs every time I went back for the holidays. The difference is, now I have a sustainable lifestyle that I actually enjoy and can maintain for the rest of my life.

My location independent office of the day

Chapter 15: Maintenance vs. Growth

The key difference between this lifestyle and every other is being able to pause and maintain whenever need be. This applies for all aspects of my life including exercise, business and even relationships. Sometimes the best way to grow and make real progress is simply to take a break from it and see if it all survives by itself. If what you had built is on a solid foundation and you put systems in place, you should be able to take 4 weeks away from it and have it survive without you; if it collapses as soon as you step away, it wasn't meant to last in the first place.

I used to dream about being able to disappear from all responsibilities and hibernate for three months at a time. I know it seems silly but I wanted nothing to do: my career, my crash diets, the workouts I forced myself to do and even the relationships I was in. I desperately wanted to escape and leave it all behind. I was unhappy and that made every inch of progress gruesome.

Now that my life is different, I actually look forward to every meal of my so-called diet, every gym session, seeing my girlfriend and even going to work. But the best thing is that, when I'm not trying to make gains and progress, everything is built on a solid enough foundation where I can simply apply maintenance mode and come back 4 or even 8 weeks later without it all falling apart.

During my ideal schedule, I have my Bulletproof coffee in the mornings, a great co-working space to work in, a brand new gym within walking distance and I live two doors down the hall from my girlfriend. Having all systems in place, it makes it incredibly easy to push forward, improve and grow.

However, just a few months ago I was on a small island in Cambodia that only had electricity for a few hours a day, no gym, and pretty much nothing I needed to work, workout or work on my relationship. The island was called Koh Rong, also known as Puppy Island, a name given to it for the sheer amount of cute puppies walking around everywhere. It had white sand beaches, warm tropical water and some of the best food I've had anywhere, served to you with the most incredible views included. I honestly can't even remember why I went to Cambodia in the first place as I didn't know anyone there and never had a huge desire to check out the country; I'm pretty sure I only went because I finally could.

I even recorded episode 16 of the Travel Like a Boss Podcast while hanging out on the beach with no internet or electricity. It wasn't the best episode but it was cool knowing that it was possible.

For my entire life previously I was either struggling to get by or just maintain my standard of living. I worked hourly, was paid a salary and everything I gained using shortcuts could be taken away just as quickly as I got them. I had been living in Thailand for four years and, even though Cambodia was right next door and dirt cheap compared to the U.S., I had never been before; however, I decided this was my year to explore. Armed with just a carry-on backpack, my Macbook Air and 2 hours of internet a day, I was able to pay for my entire trip, keep my fitness gains and even maintain my relationship while I was away.

Koh Rong, Cambodia

My schedule was to wake up at 8am and walk down to the beach with my laptop ready to crush work. Realize, though, that nothing was open until 10am, so I would walk around for two hours looking for a restaurant or coffee shop that had wifi and end up back at the place closest to me which finally turned their generators on at ten. I'd check my email, respond to any customer service inquires that came in and forward any orders to my suppliers. During maintenance mode this could all be done within half an hour; however, it usually took an hour because the internet was so slow. The good news, though, was I did it over breakfast and then had the entire rest of the day to paddle board, kayak, scuba dive, hike across the jungle or simply lay on the beach and relax.

My diet consisted of beachside BBQs or Fish Amok which is a local Cambodian dish consisting of fresh coconut milk and kroeung, a type of Khmer curry paste made from lemongrass, turmeric root, garlic, shallots, an herb called galangal and ginger. For exercise I did a few push-ups whenever I could but mainly I just kept active by doing things around the island that I enjoyed anyways.

Funnily enough, things like playing beach volleyball never appealed to me when I lived near Huntington Beach in California even though it was incredible there. I had told myself that I didn't enjoy it but secretly it was because I sucked at it, didn't look good with my shirt off and was afraid to join in with people better than me. Having no additional training and simply by being in better shape, I suddenly became good enough where I now enjoy it and jump on the opportunity whenever I see a game.

In the weeks after I left Koh Rong I continued to travel around the quiet riverside town of Kampot, which is famous for growing peppercorns, then made my way through the rest of Cambodia, stopping to see the ancient Angkor Wat temples which were magnificent by the way. In these weeks of not working for more than an hour a day - and often not opening my laptop for days at a time - never seeing the inside of a real gym or having access to healthy food, I thought I would have lost everything I had worked so hard towards for months. Yet I arrived back in Chiang Mai, resumed my routine within days and realized that not only was the month-long break a great reboot for motivation but I hadn't lost a step while gone.

I decided to try putting my life into maintenance mode again while traveling through Saigon in Vietnam and while visiting friends and family back in the U.S. Every time I left for 3 weeks or more, I would come back with more money in the bank, more inches off my waist and, surprisingly, better progress in my relationship as it gave us time to miss each other. Even friendships are often put in maintenance mode while we travel. My three closest friends are currently living in three separate countries, yet I feel like I'm closer to them than friends I had that lived in the same city as me back home. Anton, for an example, has been living in Saigon for these past 6 months while I've been based out of Chiang Mai; however, we somehow seem to hang out together more than I see some people that live minutes away from me.

Being able to travel, build and repeat has been a huge reason why I've been able to continue pushing forward and reach my goals as quickly as I have. The biggest problems with not building your foundations having the maintenance mode option is slipping back whenever you are not making forward progress. Having Chiang Mai as my home base has allowed me to travel for a few weeks or even months, maintain my fitness levels, and even my bank balance and then go back and start making huge progress again once I"m back in work mode.

Chapter 16: Written In The Air To Oslo

After a few months of being back in growth mode I'm now sitting in seat 1C and, even though there is a giant viking of a man next to me, I'm sitting comfortably having just woken up from a four hour nap. Ten rows behind me there is a curtain that separates where I am now to where I used to sit and struggle to be comfortable. It wasn't without hardships and setbacks however.

When I first started this journey, exactly one year ago, I dreamt of being able to go to Europe with my friend, Kurt. At that point, I would have flown cargo class if it saved me money. In the past, every time I would walk past the premium seats while getting off the plane, I would be tempted to sit down and see how it felt. I never did, though, as I was too embarrassed to especially since there would always be a long line of people behind me. To make myself feel better I would tell myself that it wasn't worth the extra cost but in reality it is. Our mental and physical health is extremely precious and does have a price tag - a relatively high one at that.

Having Europe as a goal helped me through setbacks which seemed to come one after another when you were down. It seems like whenever life is going well, everything goes as planned, but as soon as you hit a bump in the road, the whole world comes crashing down. I don't mention this often, but in the months right before my first sale, everything that could have went wrong, happened all at once. Punspace was my savior, and my laptop was key to success. Yet both of those things betrayed me one after another. While walking to work one morning after it had rained the night before, the wooden walkway in front of the co-working space decided to give out on me. I felt it happening in slow motion but there was nothing I could do but fall through the floor, severely cutting my right leg when it happened.

Even though health care is cheap in Thailand, I didn't even have the $60 to get stitches at the time, so I kept my leg wrapped up, applied antibiotic ointment on it daily and hoped it would heal on its own. It didn't. I was losing my health, couldn't run, or go to the gym, and thought maybe it was a blessing and took it as a sign to spend more time working on my dropshipping store. Then my laptop decided to fail on me. There I was, sitting in a co-working space, with a business to build, unable to walk more than a few blocks without pain in my leg, and with no hope in sight. The worst thing was, everyone around me was doing exceptionally well and it became harder and harder to stay positive.

The new Macbook air had just come out and everyone I knew bought one. I would eventually be one of the lucky ones but not until after a series of unpredictable events. My good friend, Nic Gregoris, who was flying to New York in a few days gave me his old Macbook Pro as a gift, as he knew I needed it. He had dropped it and the bezel was coming off but it was still the best laptop I've ever owned, until a few weeks later when the hinge finally gave out and the screen started peeling off on its own. I sent it into service to get repaired but weeks went by with me checking on it daily with no progress, eventually it would be fixed and became my favorite laptop I've ever owned, but until then, it was the kindness of a guy named Cameron Parker that got me through those few dark weeks.

I met Cameron at the co-working space and he was one of the lucky ones who was doing well enough in his business that he bought the new Macbook air without a second thought. I saw that he had posted his old HP laptop for sale and asked him if I could borrow it for a few days until I got mine back from service. I'm sure to him it wasn't a big deal, but to me his kindness was a lifesaver. I was running out of savings quick and if I didn't make my first sale soon, I might have had to give up on my dream of owning an online business and start looking for jobs again soon. It was the generosity of friends that I had met along the way that helped me make it past the treacherous path in the dark, just like it was my guide that pushed me through reaching the summit of Mt. Kinabalu just a year before that. I truly believe that the lessons I learned from pushing myself far past my comfort zones in fitness, have given me the strength to push myself past the uncertain times of being a striving entrepreneur.

Sitting here in business class typing on a dream come true, after everything I've been through to get here, I promise myself that I'll do whatever it takes to continue making enough money to never have to sit in coach again. For short flights I really don't mind sitting wherever they want to put me, especially if it allows me to fly down to the islands for the weekend with my girlfriend or pop over to see friends; however, as for flying from Thailand back to the U.S. or any other flight over 5 hours, if I can't afford to fly business class, I'll just put my head down and work until I can.

My girlfriend, being extremely new to international travel, thinks I'm insane. In her mind paying an extra $4,000 to upgrade to business class when the standard ticket was already $1,000 is just plain stupid. I agree with her - it is kind of stupid - and I wish that the price difference wasn't so drastic. However, when it comes down to it, I can either spend my energy complaining about business class being too expensive, and rationalizing to myself why I don't need it or I can just figure out how to make more money.

Yesterday was the first day I ever wrote an income report on my blog. I've seen other (much more) successful entrepreneurs do it in the past and

I've always gotten a lot out of it. If you had asked me how much money I made per month for the past 6 months I wouldn't have been able to guess. My plan of action these past 6 months has been simply to make more than I spent.

Living in Chiang Mai made that extremely easy. I live in the Nimmanhemin district of Chiang Mai, which is similar to the beloved West Village New York or SOMA in San Francisco. It's a lot more expensive than living even 10 minutes away but I love being able to walk to the gym, the mall and all of our favorite restaurants. It's also near all of the coffee shops, trendy bars and even the newest cinema, which makes it a no-brainer to want to live there.

The only reason not to live there is the price; it's exactly the same reason why a lot of people choose to live over the bridge or in the boroughs instead of in the cities of San Francisco or New York. We tell ourselves it's better value to live in Queens or in Oakland but, in reality, we would enjoy it more living in the area where we want to be instead of settling for a place that's more affordable. The problem with always looking for the best value in life is, often, that means you live a little bit less.

When I lived in San Francisco, I hardly experienced the city at all because I lived in the suburb of the Sunset District. On paper it's still technically a part of the city and it is only a 20 minute train ride from the heart of the city; however, that short train ride away gave me the excuse to stay home most weeknights and, until this day, I've only experienced the true San Francisco a few times, and that was when I got to hang out with friends who actually lived in the heart of the city.

I wish someone would have smacked me aside the head and told me there's a huge difference between acknowledging that I want to fly business class and live in the best areas of the city while simply not yet being able to afford it, and lying to myself saying it wasn't even something that I would enjoy.

If I had simply sat down in those big comfortable business class seats every time I walked past them from coach, I would have spent those years daydreaming about how I could eventually afford it, instead of wasting time rationalizing to myself that it wasn't something I wanted. It's easy to find excuses why something seemingly out of reach isn't worth reaching for anyways; however, it's much more rewarding to keep reaching for those goals as, one day, you'll wake up from a nap and realize that you're on your way to Norway sitting in seat 1C looking out at the clouds and new adventures below you.

Chapter 17: Putting In The Work.

My father was always an extremely hard worker and he prided himself on that. He must have told me a hundred times the story of how he used to wake up at 5:30am to sit in the cold and study English before going to his job at the gas station an hour later. The moral being that he worked so hard for the entire summer he stared at the Coca Cola machine and dreamt about how amazing it would taste. Just a year before that day, my dad had been a chemist in a cola factory back in Taiwan, where he had an easy life and earned a good salary.

My parents moved to the U.S. as soon as my older sister, Christina, was born hoping to give her (and the future me) a better chance at a successful life. One hot summer afternoon, my father finally decided to treat himself to a can of Coke. He was so excited to enjoy the cold refreshing beverage but, since pop-top tabs in Taiwan are different from those in the States, he accidentally tore it off instead of pushing down while trying to open the can. Instead of buying another he walked home after work, clutching that cold can of Coke, and used his tools to finally open it up. I never asked him if the Coke was warm by then or why he didn't just borrow a screwdriver from the gas station he worked at but, either way, I've heard that story of his perseverance at least a hundred times.

It wasn't that I didn't admire my dad's hard work; I just knew that I never wanted to go down that path as I didn't see it being successful. The one lesson I got out of all of my dad's hard work stories was actually to do the opposite. I prided myself on working smarter instead of harder, and loved figuring out shortcuts to get things done. I coasted through high school, college and even a career never working hard at all. My friends nicknamed me Mr. Shortcut, a title that I was extremely proud of at the time but later learned was also my curse.

It turns out that my Dad and everyone else who ever preached it was right all along - hard work really does pay off. This past year I've worked harder to build a business than I've worked at all of my previous jobs combined. I started getting to the office by 6:45am everyday even though there was no timecard to clock in. Instead of coasting through life, living the 4-hour workweek, I purposely started working 40. It's strange, I never thought I would ever do more work than necessary but hard work really has paid off. In just one year my income has grown from $600 a month to over $7,000 a month and I only see that continuing to increase.

The hard work paid off big time! But by that logic, my father should have been a millionaire yet never made more than $15 an hour. The problem was he worked hard for someone else and not for himself. This is the missing key to it all. The reason why I never worked hard at any of my corporate jobs is because I knew the effort I put in made someone else rich and only gave me pennies on the dollar for my time. Now I know that everything I do directly grows my business I'm happy to put in a million perfect effort as I know I get back million percent returns.

It's time to work smart by working for yourself - while working hard - because as your own boss you are the one to suffer or to gain.

Here since 6:45am.
I'm sitting in an empty co-working space, setting big goals and reaching them.

Chapter 18: Where The Heck Is Bucharest?

There are a lot of places in the world I have no desire to travel to and, I feel a bit stupid to say, there are even more than I've even heard of. I've been playing with the interactive map and followed the route we flew from Thailand until where we are now.

We flew over Rangoon in Burma, through Bangladesh, across the Himalayas in Nepal, Pakistan, Afghanistan and skipped over places I thought were a joke from the movie, 'Borat'. I had no idea, until now, that Uzbekistan and Turkmenistan were real countries. The Caspian Sea which we just crossed sounded like something out of 'Game of Thrones', as well as the Black Sea being something from a video game.

I admit my geography is pretty terrible and I'm extremely ill-prepared for this trip to Europe. So far on our open ended itinerary we have 5 days in Berlin and another 5 days in Budapest planned, with nothing in mind for the rest of the trip. Taking a look at the map now, Prague in the Czech Republic is exactly halfway between Budapest and Berlin so that sounds like a place I should visit as well.

The thing is, the more I start traveling and the more I open my eyes, the more places I want to go. I can't even imagine living my entire life working, and then dying, without seeing more than once place in the world. I don't remember the statistics but a big portion of Americans live and die within 25 miles of where they were born. I could have easily become one of them.

I always knew, deep down inside, that there was something wrong with the standard life plan that we were dealt but it wasn't courage that convinced me to see more of the world. In fact, it was fear and desperation. I was so unhappy at the thought of working a job for the next 40 years I didn't love, getting married to a girl who I wasn't passionate about, and being trapped, that I gave it all up and just left it all behind. I still can't believe that was almost six years ago and even had to double check just now what year it actually was. I have friends back home that dream of doing the same but they all have their own set of excuses. The most common are:

"It's different when you have kids."
and
"I can't travel because I just bought a house and have a mortgage and responsibilities."

Don't get me wrong, I still want to have kids someday and I would love to have a house to call my own. But I know that a lot of my friends wish they would have done things differently. I know this because even though they post happy photos of them at restaurants, or even photos of their baby, they all pull me aside or message me privately and ask me about what life is like being free. The other problem is, out of everyone I know who recently bought a house, almost none of them actually own their house.

Instead of simplifying their life, selling all of their stuff and traveling for a year until they figure it out, they try to find happiness by remodeling their home, buying a new car, or having another kid. They dig themselves deeper and deeper into an inescapable pit, so they then have an excuse why they can't do what they truly want to do.

I used to think they were right: that I would soon regret not saving up, buying a house, focusing on my career and getting old. Friends would often instill that fear in me every time we spoke, as a way to make themselves feel better about their lives.

Two years ago I started having my doubts and every time I went back to the U.S. I thought long and hard about settling down there again. I would tell myself that my vacation was over and that it was time to rejoin reality, and the workforce, again. I should buy a car, sign a lease and mortgage a home. Thank god I didn't because I see how miserable the majority of my friends are who have done just that. There are some who really love their new lives, their homes, have happy marriages and love being a parent. But most are stressed out, in debt, and secretly pull me aside telling me they wish they could give it all up and regain their freedom.

I just finished watching the in-flight film, '12 Years a Slave', and realized how standard life isn't that much different. We trade our time for money and are slaves to the corporations we work for and support, as well as banks, neither of which care about our well-being the least bit. It's insane to think having 2 weeks vacation a year is standard when, if you do the math, that's trading 50 weeks of work for just 2 weeks of enjoyment.

Instead, think about this: why don't we do work that we actually enjoy doing? Work that challenges us, inspires us and allows us to feel like we've accomplished something by the end of it. Let us put our effort into building something real, something that you can be proud of at the end of the day, and something that you can sell for 18x monthly profit if you ever end up wanting to walk away from it.

What does that mean?

Let us vow not to be slaves any more.

If you are unhappy with your life, just change it.

The solution is simple: first, realize that it's never the perfect time; second, realize that everyone has excuses or commitments; third, simplify your life by getting rid of everything you don't need, and use that runway to spend a year focusing on what really does make you happy.

If you hate your job - quit. If you're in a bad relationship and don't love your partner - break up. If you don't like where you live - move. It really is that simple when you don't allow yourself to give excuses. Fear is what holds us back but, in reality, there aren't that many things to truly be afraid of, even 41,000 feet above Bucharest, wherever in the world that is.

Chapter 19: Now It's Your Turn.

I wish I had all of the answers, and I wish that this book could be the universal solution to everyone's problems, and the road map to everyone's success and happiness. Everytime I get a message from a reader of '12 Weeks in Thailand', my blog or a listener of my Podcast telling me how much their life has improved since they got inspired to go after their goals, it puts a smile on my face.

However, for every person who I hear from that succeeds, I'm sure there are twenty who never even started or have already given up. We've all heard that 8 out of 10 businesses fail. If we focus on that alone maybe we should never even start. But instead, I'd rather listen to the words of someone who has actually made it happen.

"...it doesn't matter how many times you fail. It doesn't matter how many times you almost get it right. No one is going to know or care about your failures, and neither should you.

All you have to do is learn from them and those around you because... All that matters in business is that you get it right once.

Then everyone can tell you how 'lucky' you are." - Mark Cuban

What I love about the billionaire's advice is that it's true. Every failed business I've ever started, and every venture that I felt might have just been a waste of time, turned out to have given me skills and insight that I use for my successful businesses today. A lot of people think I'm lucky that my first dropshipping store I ever created made $18,000 in sales the first month but what people don't talk about are the two months that I worked at it, making $0, with no guarantee that it would ever start working. Few people also mention that the reason why I was successful with it was because I followed Anton's steps and basically just did whatever he told me to - without question. If it wasn't for him spending the last 7 years figuring it out and putting it into a course it would have taken me just as long to have figured it out for myself.

But even with all of the tools and step-by-step tutorials, a lot of people still don't become successful, and I know it's because they have their energy in the wrong places. A big part of my success financially is directly related to my success with reaching my health goals, eliminating stress and responsibilities from my life and surrounding myself with positive, open-minded people who are all striving for success themselves.

Take my friend, Ben, for an example. I met him at Tiger Muay Thai while doing jiu-jitsu and living the 'good life on the cheap' in Thailand. We lived in basic rooms with shared bathrooms at the gym for $150 a month apiece and spent our days doing Muay Thai and MMA. We had unlimited freedom of time as, after morning training, we'd often spend the rest of our afternoons hanging out at the beach. We'd sometimes even do our entire workout on the beach.

But then the vacation was over. Ben moved back to California and went back to the real world. Through keeping in touch on facebook he saw that I was looking to hire someone part time to take phone calls for my dropshipping store.
He messaged me and said he had a lot of free time on his hands and could use the extra income from answering calls for me. As much as I thought

he would be perfect for the job, work hard, and provide great customer service, I declined his application. I didn't hear from him for five months after that and thought I had lost a friend. But instead, it turned out he had taken that as a sign to start his own store instead. He signed up for the same dropshipping course that I took (www.AntonMethod.com) and started his own store.

Months later he finally responded.

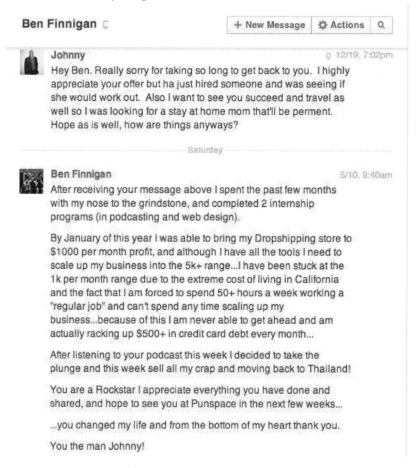

Now I'm sitting in the same co-working space as him halfway across the world. He managed to scale up the profits of his first store within weeks and is already working on his second store in his spare time. I invited him on as a guest for episode 39 of the Travel Like a Boss Podcast to hear his story on how he finally managed to make the move back out to

Thailand, and then invited him back on a week later for episode 40 to hear how much he had already accomplished since being out here.

Even with all of the tools available we often don't take advantage of them and seize the day as we should. I hope that this book provided both the tools as well as the inspiration for everyone reading this to take the first step. Whether your goals are getting in great shape, finding love and starting a family, traveling the world or starting a business, the first steps are the same: set your goals, be honest to yourself in what it will take, and be prepared to put in the sacrifice to accomplish them.

It's easy to forget that when I started this yearlong journey, it was just about the vanity of getting in shape. My sacrifice was giving up my dating life, career, Muay Thai, scuba diving, money, and whatever else would stand in my way. Somehow, by giving all of that up in the beginning of the year, I'm now ending it with an abundance of it all.

Capture the day and start by asking yourself what you've truly desired your whole life.

Ignore the naysayers, disregard logic and, for once in your life, just give it everything you've got. This very moment is the youngest we'll ever be, and every day that passes can either bring us closer to the life we've always dreamed of or put it off for another lifetime that we'll never get to see.

Life really does change quick.

Warm Regards,

www.JohnnyFD.com

Congratulations on finishing the book!

If you liked it, please do me a HUGE favor and give it a 5 star review on Amazon.

---

1 of 1 people found the following review helpful

★★★★★ **EXCELLENT SOURCE OF INFORMATION & A REALLY FUN READ!!!**, June 25, 2014

By **Nick from Vega$** (Las Vegas, NV) - See all my reviews

Verified Purchase (What's this?)

This review is from: **12 Weeks in Thailand: The Guide Book to Travel Cheap, Learn Muay Thai all while Living the 4-Hour Workweek (Kindle Edition)**

I've been planning my dream trip to Thailand for many years. I've been putting it off due to fear of the unknown, and not knowing where to start. Johnny does an awesome job of providing detailed information on travelling, expenses, places to visit, and so much more.

His personal stories were VERY interesting too! Some of the stuff he shares about dating was like reading a private diary! It was cool of him to open up, and allow us into his personal experiences.

I would highly recommend this book to anyone who has the itch to travel to Thailand. I am thankful to Johnny for sharing his priceless information with us.

Thanks Johnny! I look forward to reading more about your adventures and successes on your blogsite [...]
I've also been religiously following all of your amazing, and truly informative podcasts on your site [...]

Help other customers find the most helpful reviews | Report abuse | Permalink

Was this review helpful to you? (Yes) (No)   Comment

---

1 of 1 people found the following review helpful

★★★★★ **Breaks is down**, June 23, 2014

By **Riley Bennett** - See all my reviews

Verified Purchase (What's this?)

This review is from: **12 Weeks in Thailand: The Guide Book to Travel Cheap, Learn Muay Thai all while Living the 4-Hour Workweek (Kindle Edition)**

Wish I'd read Johnny's book before I visited for 2 weeks last year. He just breaks it down for you - everything you should know. Reading this book helped me gain the confidence to return for an extended stay. Also following his blog gave me good ideas for making income while i'm there. Good book from a real dude.

Help other customers find the most helpful reviews | Report abuse | Permalink

Was this review helpful to you? (Yes) (No)   Comment

If you haven't already, make sure you read my first book:

12 Weeks in Thailand: The Good Life on the Cheap
(www.12WeeksinThailand.com)

Topics include:

- Costs of Living in Thailand
- Travel on the Cheap
- How to live off of $600 or less a month
- The single life in Thailand
- Working as a Professional Scuba Diver
- Living and Training at Muay Thai/MMA Gyms

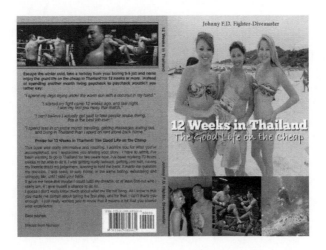

How to Keep in Touch:

I love hearing success stories and meeting up for a coconut with anyone who makes it out to Thailand or wherever else I am in the world at the time.

Find me at www.facebook.com/johnnyfdk

Tweet me @johnnyfdk

Stay informed:

As much as I love laying around poolside, I'm always up to something new. Stay a part of the journey and join me as Life Changes Quick.

Listen to the podcast at: www.TravelLikeaBossPodcast.com

Read my blog at: www.JohnnyFD.com

Did I ever make it out to Europe?

Yes I did! And it was incredible! Check out my blog for mini guides to each country I visited, packed full of photos and short videos at www.JohnnyFD.com

Tell your friends to check out the book at:

www.LifeChangesQuick.com

Thanks for reading, I sincerely hope you enjoyed this book as well as got something out of it. -Johnny

7531028R00071

Printed in Great Britain
by Amazon.co.uk, Ltd.,
Marston Gate.